simply pink

PAULA PRYKE
simply pink

jacqui small

photography by Polly Wreford

For Elizabeth and Anne
and all those who know the magic of pink!

First published in 2009 by
Jacqui Small LLP,
7 Greenland Street
London NW1 0ND

Text copyright
© Paula Pryke 2009
Photography, design and
layout copyright
© Jacqui Small 2009

Publisher Jacqui Small
Editorial Manager Lesley Felce
Designer Maggie Town
Editor Sian Parkhouse
Production Peter Colley

ISBN 978 1 906417 21 5

A catalogue record for this book is available
from the British Library.

2011 2010 2009

10 9 8 7 6 5 4 3 2 1

Printed in China

contents

my passion for pink

MY LOVE AFFAIR with the colour pink started in childhood but has endured and intensified as I have matured. I still prefer pink to any other colour. There is something about the colour that intrigues me. It has such a wide colour spectrum and I find I have a very emotional reaction to it. At one level it soothes and beguiles me and makes me feel just a little more rosy inside. It is a happy colour, a fun colour and above all a slightly magical colour. It can be calming, soothing and gentle or it can be outrageous, loud and arresting. Pink can suggest many things: femininity, youthfulness, innocence, delicacy, romance and yet it can also be very dominant, bold and sexy!

I feel extremely privileged to be able to work professionally with flowers and one of the most motivating forces for me is working with the colours of nature. In our everyday life we are now very influenced by the colour trends of the season. Colour predictors may suggest seasonal colours that reflect world events and the mood of the times and marketing gurus may more cynically present others to us.

Whatever the trends for the last few years, working so closely with clients' colour choices I can confirm that for the last five years we have been going through a very pink phase, with it being by far the most requested colour and the preferred wedding choice. As a result of its popularity, there has been an enormous influx of new varieties of flowers produced for the cut-flower trade in the pink colour spectrum. We are definitely currently in the pink, and long may it continue!

ABOVE Pink ranunculus – my favourite flower.

pink inspirations

THIS PAGE My pink cottage garden favourites include *Clematis* 'Anna', *Cirsium rivulare* 'Atropurpureum', valerian, foxgloves, lupins, 'Handel' and 'Gertrude Jekyll' roses and the candy pink *Campanula medium* 'Champion Pink', with some stems of honeysuckle.

garden bounty

FOR THE LAST FOUR YEARS I have been living outside London and re-connecting with gardening. I am not a good garden designer because I want to have one of everything and I like my garden to be so packed with flowers that it is like walking through one of my arrangements. I also prefer it to be slightly wild and natural, too, and I tend to let the dominant plants have their way with the weaker ones rather than imposing my own will. These collections of pink flowers were harvested from my own patch in the early morning before the commute to London. Valerian is a self-sown flower in my garden, but I have come to love it since I have found it to be such a useful filler for my flower arrangements, and it has a good vase life. Honeysuckle is a passion, and I have at least five different varieties in my garden, but it does not last well as a cut flower.

TOP RIGHT I think clematis is very underrated as a cut flower – here the pale pink variety 'Anna' is arranged with lupins and valerian.

MAIN PICTURE I am a huge admirer of foxgloves, particularly when they grow wild and are not under the watchful eye of a gardener. These tall spires of quite exotic looking, delicate bell-shaped flowers with spotted throats make good seasonal cut flowers in late spring and early summer.

RIGHT The quintessential English rose, 'Gertrude Jekyll' is simply the best. I love the colour and the shape.

'Roses are incredibly sensual and I would not be without them in my garden'

my favourite rose

IT IS VERY HARD FOR ME to offer up just one favourite pink rose when there are so many I adore and order from my suppliers each week, but one that has endured and been constant for the last 15 years or so is the South American rose 'Anna'. It has a very lovely shape and colour and the inside of the rose is just slightly paler than the outside. It reminds me of the highest quality ice cream – the colour is so attractive it looks creamy and almost good enough to eat! South American roses are packed in 25s rather than the usual 20s and they are usually rather less uniform in length. Their heads are packed at different heights to make maximum room for the air freight and when they are unpacked they need reviving by re-cutting about 5cm (2in) off the bottom of the stem with a diagonal cut, and letting them regain their strength in water mixed with flower food with their packaging still on. After 24 hours we remove the packaging and any outer petals of the rose head that have been damaged by the wrapping. They look just perfect massed together on their own.

OPPOSITE A large hand-tied posy of 'Anna' roses – the perfect bouquet to celebrate the arrival of a baby girl.

THIS PAGE The colour variation is what makes 'Anna' so perfect to me, with its gradations from the creamy bud opening into pink outer petals.

THIS PAGE Everlasting pea, feverfew, blackberry, valerian, wild teasels, cow parsley, sweet cicely, pink veronica and musk mallow are each given their own milk bottle vase, and the collection is bound together with gardener's twine.

wild flower hunt

IN RETROSPECT I think my obsession with flowers started when I was about five or six when I picked wild flowers in the water meadows around my parents' home in Suffolk. Observing flowers in the wild is a huge inspiration for me and it leads to a more holistic approach to flower arranging. The shape of the flower, its habitat and the way that it is mixed with other colours have all informed my work. While out walking if you come across a carpet of bluebells or a scattering of foxgloves in a leafy glade you are struck by the power of massing one type of flower together. The simplicity of flowers in nature is also arresting and always central to my work. For me the simpler the design the better it is, as you are drawn more to the stars of the arrangement, the flowers themselves. The natural curiosity of a child to collect a group of random flowers and place them together in an old jam jar is simplicity at its best.

THIS PAGE It is amazing what treasures a countryside walk can yield. This collection of self-sown garden and wild flowers demonstrates that Mother Nature is as big a fan of the colour pink as I am!

One of the joys of working with flowers is that there are always new varieties appearing, and with the change of the seasons there is a constant roving menu of plant material. This helps to keep my work fresh and evolving. Every now and then a new rose comes along and leads you to new combinations. This dusky pink 'Two Faces+' rose has been a recent muse.

paisley pinks

THE SETTING AND INTERIOR of a room is central to the selection of plant material and containers. Table linen in particular is often chosen in collaboration with the flowers' decorations, sometimes to match or tone, and always to make the most of the central arrangement. On some occasions I may be sent a swatch of fabric for a bridesmaid's dress or for a tablecloth from an event planner, and I will take it along to the wholesale flower market early in the morning and begin to collect flowers and foliages that complement the swatch. When the event is in a marquee or a simple room like a modern museum you can often use patterned cloths to great effect because the interior is essentially blank and does not fight with the table linen. Sometimes the colours and the style of the fabric will more directly affect my choice of design. Here the swirl pattern of the paisley invited me to use a curly sage green boat container and then use a collection of very textural and blowsy shapes to fill it.

rustic jugs and cans

I HAVE OFTEN BEEN ASKED which comes first in the design process, the container or the flowers. In my own home I nearly always choose the flowers and then select the vase from my vast collection. However, often a selection of flowers will suggest a particular type of vase or the container itself will inspire me to put together a design. Rustic jugs and watering cans are great inspirational forces and invite me to spiral cottage favourites into country bunches. I also love old cooking pots and jars, particularly in earthy tones, such as antique oil pots from the Provence region of France or vintage earthenware kitchen bowls. Antique carafes and jars can also make great vases. Many of these containers have wide bases and narrower tops, which are the best shape for hand-tied bouquets and display the flower heads well.

OPPOSITE I filled this pink enamelled watering can with blue and pink love-in-a-mist (the pink variety *Nigella* 'Pink Power' is new as a cut flower), *Astilbe* 'Erica', pale pinks stocks, a new variety of pale lilac scabious and a new double daisy *Aster* 'Pink Pearl'.

THIS PAGE I love the shape of this enamel jug which, when filled, has a wide enough mouth to create a good spread of flowers. Here it is filled with *Alchemilla mollis*, *Consolida ajacis*, rose-coloured eustoma, two-tone antirrhinum and the wonderful scented garden rose 'Evelyn'.

THIS PAGE A hand-tied posy of 'Barcelona' tulips, aqua-packed in cellophane, sits in a sequinned bag. We make lots of this type of arrangement for bridesmaids' posies, as they are easy to carry. Pink roses would work equally well in this bag.

bags and baskets

FLOWERS HAVE BEEN ARRANGED in baskets since the beginnings of modern floristry, which has its origins in the early 20th century. Baskets were originally an inexpensive natural container made from bamboo or willow that complemented the flowers. Arranging flowers in bags became fashionable about ten years ago when it became a new way to market 'to-go' flowers. At about the same time, bags filled with flowers for special events and weddings became a new take on an old theme and one that has become very central to my trademark look. Taking new accessories and using them to originate new flower arrangements has added a very feminine look to my work, and these accessories have contributed greatly to the inspiration of new designs.

THIS PAGE The brightly toned woven basket was filled with the guelder rose *Viburnum opulus* 'Roseum', asters and 'Cristian' spray roses. This is an ideal gift to take with you if you are arriving at an event, as the hostess needs to do nothing other than display it and admire it!

LEFT This sequinned flower handbag captivated me, as flower shapes are a very important inspiration in my designs. Here the round shape of a daisy whose petals radiate from one central point had inspired a handbag designer.

OPPOSITE This was my interpretation of the daisy bag in flowers. A posy of pink carnations *Dianthus* 'Farida' encircles an echinops head studded with pink pearl-headed pins – a design in which nature imitates fashion imitating nature!

carnival ribbons

THE COLOURS and textures of ribbon have always drawn me and from very early days I remember being fascinated by art shops and old haberdashers with their drawers of coloured embroidery silks. Most recently this interest in ribbons brought me into contact with designer Isabel Stanley, who creates amazing lampshades using strips of ribbon. I connected very personally with her use of colour and this drew me to her studio, not far from mine in central London, where she made me some bespoke vase covers for corporate events and for my studio. The talented work of many designers in lots of different media often fires my own imagination. Over the years I have had the chance to collaborate with a number of vase designers, and I find that many individually designed pieces take a central place in my own home. I use these pink ribbon vases for my bedroom.

OPPOSITE, MAIN PICTURE AND INSET ABOVE I was given these carnival headdresses at the San Antonio Children's Fiesta in Texas, and they have often inspired me to use long ribbons in my fresh headdress designs.

OPPOSITE, INSET BELOW I love the textures and finishes of these ribbons, and I have spools of them in my studio.

THIS PAGE This vase is filled with *Stephanandra*, *Cotinus coggygria* 'Royal Purple', *Lilium* 'Medusa', *Paeonia lactifolium* 'Karl Rosenfield', trailing amaranthus, *Dahlia* 'Karma Choc' and the small *Allium sphaerocephalon*.

THIS PAGE Pink aquatic aggregates have been swirled into this glass fishbowl and then topped with a spiralled hand-tied posy of green amaranthus, blue 'Whisper' eryngiums, Germini gerberas, *Alchemilla mollis*, garden roses and a collar of the coral fern *Gleichenia polypodioides*. Wired seashells have been placed through the design with pink reel wire.

OPPOSITE Nature is a great teacher and inspiration about colour, texture and good design, no more so than in a collection of perfectly formed seashells.

seashells and sand

PICKING UP SEASHELLS on the beach is as natural to me as picking wild flowers while on a walk. Their textures, colours and shapes are fascinating and their natural tones work well with plant material. I often like to work with them on their own and, using a glue gun, will make them into wreaths. At Christmas time we often gild them and add shells to trees, garlands and seasonal wreaths. Using sand, stones and other aggregates is an inexpensive way of customizing a container in a colour or a pattern, as shown here. A cylinder-shaped glass vase was placed into a fishbowl. The gap was filled with swirls of coloured aggregates and sand and then a few special shells were wired into a hand-tied design.

THIS PAGE A selection of sweets
that make perfect partners for pink
flowers: bon-bons, alphabet sweets,
flying saucers and jellybeans.

OPPOSITE A straight-sided glass dish
was filled with an inner liner containing
floral foam and filled with coloured
mints. The flowers include 'Revival',
'Prima Donna' and 'Ilios!' roses, pink
veronica, pink and peach ranunculus,
'Gipsy Queen' hyacinths and green
amaranthus. The little green balls are the
flax *Linum usitatissimum* – this is grown
mostly for dried flower supply.

sweeties

I HAVE BEEN USING SWEETS as accessories to my designs for well over 15 years. I think I am drawn to the colours and the combination they offer, which is either very pastel or can be very artificial if a lot of food dye has been used. Mostly we use the pastel colours for weddings and christenings and the more brightly coloured sweets for bar mitzvahs. Sometimes we use the sweets on their own. I once decorated a family and friends Christmas party for a major banking group at the Royal Opera House in Covent Garden, London, using just a lorry load of those quintessentially British sweets 'Liquorice Allsorts' and lots of hot glue. I recently made cones of brightly coloured hard-boiled sweets for the children's tables of a bar mitzvah, while the highly dyed harlequin-coloured Happy roses were used en masse on all the adult tables.

pink
by design

LEFT Single heads of bright pink ranunculus are arranged in small water-holding phials in delicate banana skin bags, allowing the innate beauty of the flower form to be highlighted.

RIGHT Posies of ranunculus edged with galax leaves are ready for two lucky bridesmaids to carry. Ranunculus can make a great alternative to roses for wedding flowers as they have greater longevity and hold their shape well.

favourite flowers

What first attracted me to change my career to one in floristry was the love of flowers, pure and simple, both in my garden and in the countryside, as well as more exotic cut flowers. Not surprisingly, many of my favourites are available in many shades of pink.

RANUNCULUS These pretty blooms have remained in the top position as my favourite flower since I started to work professionally with flowers over 20 years go. Initially I was attracted to the multicoloured mix of brightly coloured ranunculus grown in Cornwall that arrive in Covent Garden around the time of my birthday in late April. Over the years these flowers have been improved enormously by hybridization and I adore the large-headed pink Clooney and the spotted Cappuccino varieties.

The main reason for my obsession with these blooms is that they are at their most graceful and gorgeous the day before they expire. When you first place ranunculus in water they are simply a bunch of wild-looking stems with good-looking tight, round blooms. After 24 hours in water they will start to re-arrange themselves, drawn by the sunlight, into a more gorgeous design and their heads start to swell a little. By the end of the week they will have opened fully, then the petals unfold and take on a translucency as if they are about to take off from the stem. I think they look better and better each day and then, just when they reach their most beautiful, they are gone, reminding me always of the transient beauty of the natural world.

'The scent of sweet peas is the quintessential
fragrance of the English summer'

SWEET PEA The English Romantic poet John Keats described these beautiful flowers: '*Here are sweet peas, on tip-toe for a flight: | With wings of gentle flush o'er delicate white, | And taper fingers catching at all things, | To bind them all about with tiny rings.*' Growing sweet peas is a perennial pleasure because they have such an interesting habit and they produce handfuls of beautiful fragrant flowers for several months.

As a cut flower they have been enormously improved and the single-coloured bunches that are sold commercially are treated post-harvest to give them greater longevity in the vase and engender them less susceptible to petal loss. For the florist, sweet peas start around Valentine's Day, with a peak in the middle of the year before they start to disappear in September.

ABOVE Sweet peas can get a little lost when mixed with other flowers so I prefer to use them on their own, massed together for their scent; on this occasion the whole arrangement was repeated for maximum impact.

ROSE There are so many varieties of roses available commercially each week, and in the last three years there has been a huge development in the range of pink roses on sale. At the cerise end of the scale I love 'Milano', a long-lasting and tall pink rose that perfectly suits gloriosa lilies. 'Aqua!' is a mid-pink rose, which has been developed especially for the trade and does not have any thorns, is a huge time-saver for busy florists. Large-headed 'Sweet Avalanche+' is a favourite pale rose and perfect for weddings. The aptly named 'Barbie' is the perfect colour for little girls, as is 'Ballet',

being stronger and more the colour of bubble gum than a tutu. New mid-pink large-headed roses which are among my favourites are 'Revival', 'Luxuria!', 'Keano' and 'Lyvera!'. 'Belle Rose' is a subtle honey-pink rose with a darker pink centre and 'Two Faces+' is a dusty brown rose that is hugely popular. There are also some fabulous spray roses in the pink range. 'Pepita' is pale pink, with 'Magic Pepita' and 'Romantic Pepita' being stronger colours. 'Lovely Lydia' is a peach-pink spray rose and 'Mimi Eden' is cream on the outside and pink inside, and most resembles a garden rose.

LEFT A selection of pink and red roses demonstrates the beauty of the flower: a neat domed hand-tied bouquet of 'Grand Prix', 'Milano' and 'Cool Water!' roses is edged with curled aspidistra leaves.

RIGHT 'Blue Pacific', 'Amalia', 'Grand Prix' and 'Titanic' roses are edged with camellia leaves and a woven collar of intertwined red Iranian dogwood and green broom. Swirls of green wire orbit the bunch to give a wilder look.

GERBERA Although gerberas are not such personal favourites as the other flowers in this section I have included them because they come up time and time again in my work. They are available in so many wonderful colours, of which pink is one amazing example. You can buy a gerbera in just about any shade of pink any week of the year. It can be used in all types of floristry and, with the smaller germini varieties as well, there are over 150 colours to select from.

MAIN PICTURE Individual Germini gerberas repeated in small tank vases make an inexpensive floral statement. These colourful daisies, which originated in Africa, are now grown in all the major flower-producing regions of the world all year round.

INSET This massed topiary of pink gerberas is a less expensive way of achieving a lot of impact at an event. Here a base of eucalyptus and skimmia are the background for these showy pink flowers. They have been raised off the table using a spray painted birch pole.

favourite flowers **43**

LEFT The muted tones of pale pink with dusty pinks and browns is one one of my favourite combinations in mid-summer. Here 'Sarah Bernhardt' peonies are hand tied with brown 'Amnésia', pale pink 'Sweet Avalanche+' and dusty pink 'Two Faces+' roses, a mixture of poppy seed heads, photinia, *Alchemilla mollis* and green dill *Anethum graveleons*. A little pink water dye has been added to the fishbowl to give a rosy glow.

shades of pink

It is the versatility in the shades of pink that make it the most important colour for me in my floral designing. Mixing the right colours is like carefully choreographing a group of dancers to create someting that is both graceful and entertaining. It's relatively easy to do the first, but making a combination achieve the second is either an innate skill or gift, or it can be the process of long endeavour, and trial and error.

SOFTLY SOFTLY We can all follow the recipe for cupcakes but some people's just taste so much better than others'. With experience you get to learn good combinations, but for me all the fun is in creating new ones and not always using the same safe selections. When arranging soft tones you have to be very careful to balance the intensity of each colour or be clever with your use of foliage to accentuate each colour value. Once you mix white into a combination it becomes very diluted, so I like to use it either quite strongly, as in the striped design, or to use it with just one colour. In a pink and white arrangement be careful to make sure the pink is less dominant so that it does not distract the eye too much.

RIGHT I always feel slightly wary of specifying Japanese knotweed from the Dutch auction after reading how invasive it has been as an imported plant – however it does have a great texture when the stems are cut. Here small lengths have been used to edge a Perspex tray of 'Avalanche+', pink 'Sweet Avalanche+' and 'Peach Avalanche+' roses.

LEFT 'Pink Cappuccino' ranunculus, 'Marshmallow' and 'Barbie' roses and 'First Class' tulips have been mixed with the white spring blossom of *Viburnum tinus*. The vase is lined with the cushiony shapes of marshmallows.

SUGAR CANDY PINKS Working with a candy-pink colour palette is a more delicate art than with pastel shades or pinks from the loud range of colour. Pink is at its prettiest and most feminine when it is in mid palette and I am particularly inspired by this in early spring when the blossom is out and there are lots of great tulips and ranunculus to use, and also again in mid summer when the peonies, sweet peas, campanula and stocks all start to beguile me. The soft tones work well on their own or when lifted and accentuated by the use of dark foliages or lighter and brighter hues. They love grey foliage and they also adore lime green. You have to be very careful not to use too much white, as that saps the subtleties, and you also have to be very wary of yellow and any variegated foliages. In a mixed palette, using more than two colours, I would leave out the white, preferring cream or vanilla as they are more subtle and complementary.

THIS PAGE I adore these 'Gertrude Jekyll' roses mixed with 'Prima Donna' and 'Super Green' roses, sprigs of lime-green *Alchemilla mollis*, pale blue nigella, candy pink nerines, campanula and 'Sarah Bernhardt' peonies. Here the palette of the sweet sherbet 'Flying Saucers' has inspired the colour of these summer flowers.

HOT PINKS The brightest and most garish pink is always the most fun! It's the slightly outrageous relative, the one that pushes the boundaries too far. The one that most people love or hate. It knows no mediocrity, it's in your face. It is the adolescent of the pink family. It demands attention and takes no hostages, only prisoners. I adore this pink and I find this colour invaluable as an accent colour. I don't want to surround myself with it, but I do need a little burst of it every now and then. I love hot pink roses, peonies, celosia, gerberas, dahlias and, most of all, exotic tendrils of climbing gloriosa heads.

LEFT Bright pink 'Serena' gerberas, gloriosia, 'Milano' roses and sprigs of fuchsia pink sisal have been added in heavy groups to a ring around a glass bowl. The pink is contrasted against orange roses and leucospermums, purple eustoma and silver brunia and coral fern foliages. Birds of paradise flowers and twisted willow stems add height.

RIGHT Grouping flowers together is one way to make more dramatic colour combinations. Here pink 'Barbie' and peach 'Prima Donna' roses have been mixed with photinia foliage, *Viburnum opulus* 'Roseum', blue hyacinths and bright pink celosia.

BRIGHT PINK MIXES EASILY WITH ANY COLOUR My favourite combinations tend to change with the season. In spring I major on bright pink with lilacs, pale blue and acid greens. As the summer unfolds I use a lot more pink with purple and deep blue. By the time we get to midsummer I tend to go for even brighter combinations, mixing sunflowers with bright pink roses, celosia and gloriosa, adding green dill and yellow achillea into the mix. Autumn time I will be drawn to using pink with orange and purples, and at Christmas I use bright pink with red and orange. If you add gold to this combination you get a rich but modern look for your festive arrangements.

OPPOSITE PAGE: ABOVE LEFT Pink bouvardia, cymbidium orchids, calla lilies and mid-pink 'Beauty by Oger' roses have been added to viburnum blossom and ivy berries in a glass vase lined with slices of cut lime. ABOVE RIGHT Dried lavender has been tied around a basket and then topped with a creamy mixture of garden roses in pinks and creams. BELOW LEFT Bright pink 'Milano' roses, *Celosia argentea* var. *cristata* 'Bombay Pink' and 'Aisha' gerberas are contrasted with orange flower heads and arranged in a bowl of sliced oranges.
BELOW RIGHT A perennially favourite colour combination of pink, lilac and green. Pink dahlias, roses, eustoma, hydrangea and astilbe are spiralled with green *Viburnum opulus* 'Roseum', fountain grasses and *Alchemilla mollis*.

THIS PAGE Big blowsy 'Kansas' peonies have been mixed with celosia and 'Serena' gerberas, with cream peonies and lime-green viburnum and *Alchemilla mollis* to give this a fresh and vibrant summer feel.

floral drama

Massing flowers together or heavily grouping them creates great visual impact and is a key way to create contemporary-feeling arrangements.

CREATING HEIGHT A tall vase is essential for making a dramatic display. These can either be used on a pedestal to give further height or they can be placed on the centre of a table to create a grand impression at a party or special venue. Ideally for tables I tend to use clear glass vases with thin stems, so a fluted glass shape is my preferred vase. I often decorate it with fruit, sweets or petals and use layers of cellophane in between which, when filled with water, gives the effect of ice.

THIS PAGE Groups of elegantly curving *Nectarscordum siculum, Anthurium* 'Nexia' tucked into the top of the vase and *Zantedeschia* 'Aurora' tied with banana rope dyed bright pink create an arrestingly sculptural display.

THIS PAGE 'Pink Panther' and 'Karl Rosenfield' peonies are interspersed with *Alchemilla mollis* and trails of asparagus fern. To add further texture and colour, the clear glass vase has been layered with cherries and faux summer berries, alternated with cut clear cellophane.

LEFT Scented stocks, massed together with a collar of twisted allium stems, demonstrate their full palette of pinks through to purple. Although you can buy stocks all the year round they are less expensive in their natural season, which is in July in the UK.

OPPOSITE, LEFT Phalaenopsis orchids hand-tied with monstera leaves are balanced on the top of a vase filled with cut phalaenopsis heads and coiled decorative pink aluminium wire.

OPPOSITE, RIGHT One of my favourite vases is this slightly flared cylinder vase, as it is a very elegant shape. I have collected them over the years in many colours and we have them in clear glass, white, black and pale pink. Here a big 'football' sphere of green floral foam has been placed onto the top of the vase and then filled with pale pink to mid-pink 'Heaven', 'Barbie', 'Blushing Akito', 'Video' and cream 'Talea+' roses.

MASSED IMPACT In the wild if you see a mass of one type of wild flower it is very arresting. The site of a carpet of buttercups in a meadow, a field of bright red poppies, a swirl of ox-eye daisies on the side of a motorway, all make very dramatic eye-catching displays. In the same way the use of one type of flower en masse for an event is very impressive. Two flowers that we use very often in this way are roses and phalaenopsis orchids. Roses work well because they can create quite sculptural effects and with the range of colours available you can always find one to match your event. Phalaenopsis orchids do not combine visually with other flowers, but look stunning and simply opulent when hand-tied together and used in tall glass vases. When flowers are in their natural season you can often buy them much more cheaply, and so this is a good time to try out the massed look without breaking the bank.

LEFT This large glossy pink urn is filled with flowering pink rhododendron, hydrangea, white lilac, spiraea, gladioli, larkspur, hanging amaranthus, dicentra, peonies and the guelder rose *Viburnum opulus* 'Rosuem'.

RIGHT Tall spires of pale pink *Eremurus* rise from a dome of pink 'Amalia','Two Faces+' and 'Blushing Akito' roses.

GRAND DESIGNS For large arrangements you generally need to order longer length flowers or create some structure to secure flower heads onto. For huge installations this may be a purpose-made structure such as an arch or a topiary shape. But if you wish to create a large arrangement using natural flowers for an urn on a pedestal or vase you will need to specify tall flowers. At most times of the year there are lots of flowers 80-100cm (30–40in) tall, and on a trip to the huge flower auctions in the Netherlands at any time of the year visitors will be amazed by the sheer range in sizes on offer in many varieties. Usually for a more traditional design one would start to get height and volume by using some very tall foliages, establishing an outline with the greenery first, and then adding the flowers. I often begin with tall spires of flowers such as pink gladioli, maybe delphinium or larkspur, and then working in the larger-headed focal flowers, such as peonies and hydrangea, and finally the fillers to lighten dark spaces in the arrangement.

decorative containers

One of my trademarks has been to use containers that were not originally intended for flowers. Platters, fruit bowls, handbags and even lampshades are all everyday objects that I have used in my floral designs, most frequently in pink!

CROCKERY Twenty years ago the containers for flower arranging were very defined. They were site specific or range specific and were usually more decorative than practical. The necks were too thin for great flower arrangements and in the main the proportions were too mean for a decent bunch of flowers. Many were actually not conducive to good flower arranging because they were too fussy or decorative. Vases were designed by potteries without much thought of how the flower arranger was going to create a good design. Some ceramic vases were designed by great floral designers, such as Constance Spry in the mid-20th century, but as this was before floral foam had been invented most relied on the use of chicken wire or had a flower rose inside to help position the flowers. The use of foam and hand-tying of flowers has opened up the possibilities for arrangements and any shape can now be filled with the use of contemporary techniques and floral sundries.

RIGHT A simple flower bottle from ceramics designer Emma Bridgewater, appropriately decorated with the words 'pink flowers', makes the perfect partner for a natural arrangement of 'Kansas' peonies.

FAR RIGHT A group of plain white mugs – the type that most of us have in our kitchen cupboard – looks stunning when filled with domed hand-tied posies of multi-hued sweet William.

'The perfect container is like the perfect outfit — you find it when you are not actually looking for it'

LEFT The soft tones of this pale pink Provençal cooking bowl inspired this arrangement of *Cosmos* 'Black Beauty', carnations, ligularia leaves, blackberries and 'Sweet Avalanche+' roses.

BELOW The perfect desk accessory – *Dianthus* 'Farida' with *Alchemilla mollis*, 'Leila' Germini gerberas and *Origanum* 'Gijsie' in an iconic Pantone pink mug.

PANTONE®
239 C

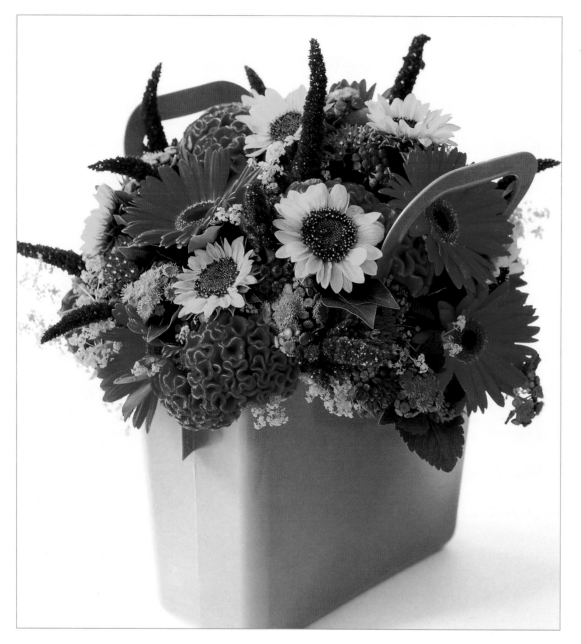

LEFT A moulded pink plastic shopper is filled with red upright amaranthus, mini sunflowers, *Ageratum houstonianum* 'Blue Horizon', *Celosia argentea* var. *cristata* 'Bombay Pink' and *Asclepias* 'Red Antonia' for a fun modern look.

BASKETS It is quite amazing to think that only about 20 years ago the main containers for flower arrangements for special occasions were baskets. These were mostly inexpensive blond bamboo baskets made in China and people who received a lot of flowers always had a massive collection of flower baskets that had been used only once. In the main at that time they had long handles for carrying and were a feature of home, wedding and even funeral flowers. I am always on the look out for quirky equivalents to give an old theme a new look, and improvements in dying techniques have led to a huge variety of colour in baskets. The expansion of plastic manufacturing has also given birth to lots of other highly coloured products that hold water and make great containers for flower designs.

RIGHT A deep pink woven bamboo basket is filled with *Chenopodium quinoa* 'Carina', *Nigella* 'Pink Power', *Alchemilla mollis*, cotinus foliage and *Asclepias* 'Amalia'.

LEFT This summer urn is filled with huge 'Coral Charm' peonies, grouped 'Amalia', 'Marrakech', and 'Peppermint' roses, with *Viburnum opulus* berries, *Photina x fraseri* 'Red Robin' and *Astrantia major* 'Claret' as the filler material.

URNS Urns and flower arrangements go together rather like the egg and spoon. You can see in museums all over the world how urns and vases have evolved and there is lots to inspire the flower arranger. Most urns have a rustic feel, being made from stone, iron or terracotta, and this is very sympathetic to plant material. Many of the ones we use for weddings are now made from fibreglass so they are lighter to move about than traditional urns, and there are also lots of new plastic versions on the market. Heavy metal urns are suitable to anchor heavy constructions such as the topiaries shown on these pages. I also find that heavy table urns are useful because they raise the flowers up in the centre of the table so they are not obscured by the wine and water glasses. Also their weight makes them less attractive to take home at the end of the event when we are trying to recover all our props! The classic urn shape is also now made in glass and recently there have been lots of coloured versions, including the bright pink one seen on page 56.

RIGHT Pink can give a traditional Christmas spruce topiary a modern twist: waxed pink apples, gilded cones, *Viburnum tinus* berries and sprigs of red skimmia and pink heads of hellebores top a heavy gilded iron urn.

FAR RIGHT Ornamental kales, camellia leaves and skimmia form the base of this conical topiary, with pale pink 'Sweet Avalanche+' and 'Aqua!' roses and wired miniature aubergines forming the colour accents. Wands of pussy willow add shape and structure.

pink events

BRIDAL BOUQUETS In recent years the overwhelming flower of choice for the bride's bouquet has been roses, and in the main the preferred option has been for a neat, round, lightweight tied bunch in one colour, often in white or ivory to match the bridal gown. Personally I prefer a colour against most bridal fabrics, especially white or ivory, as it makes a better statement and I feel colour makes the overall effect warmer and prettier; pink is perfect for this. If you do not feel that you can go for a strong colour then there are all kinds of ways of introducing a hint of colour without going the full way. For silvery or grey dress fabric an accent of silver foliage, which is slightly reflective, is a great way of enhancing the compatibility of the flowers with the gown.

Country weddings suit a little colour and I love to do two or three colour bouquets for spring and summer casual weddings. Muscari is a very beautiful wedding flower as its shape is so delicate. The colour combines well with pink, and is as soothing as the colour of a perfect blue sky! In this bouquet it is combined with 'Blushing Akito' roses and blue nigella.

LEFT A posy of 'Two Faces+' roses is aqua-packed in a satin and marabou-trimmed handbag, with a confetti cone of petals and pink sugared almond favours. Even the tiniest of bridesmaids would find this easy to carry down the aisle.

OPPOSITE This delightful bridesmaid's pomander of 'N-joy' rose heads was massed on a floral foam base and finished with a lacy ribbon trim.

BRIDESMAIDS' POSIES You can have a little fun with the bridesmaids' flowers by making them a slightly more unusual shape or by adding accessories. I love to use little bags or coloured baskets, which are easy to carry, or an interesting trim, such as a pretty satin ribbon binding or marabou feather trim for a real touch of glamour. Pomanders are lovely, too, for bridesmaids in the 7 to 12 age range. If the maids are younger than that the pomanders can be rather too heavy and get picked up and put down too often, which damages the flower heads. Roses are the easiest to use in small round spherical balls of foam. With mixed flowers it is more difficult to achieve a perfect ball shape, so I recommend picking one type of flower with uniform-sized heads. Soft stems such as spring flowers are more difficult to use and really require wiring, which is not an amateur sport! I think you cannot beat simple hand-tied posies of one type of flower, and my favourites would be pink ranunculus, peonies, sweet peas or roses.

A floral foam ring around a glass pink candelabra is edged with *Alchemilla mollis* and ivy berries and topped with pink and burgundy dahlias with bright pink 'Karl Rosenfield' peonies, 'Milano' roses and gloriosa lilies. The cube vase seen on the table beyond is filled with a hand-tied posy of the same combination. The Arne Jacobsen chairs have very sexy tight cerise chair covers made by a fashion designer friend, John Crummay.

WEDDING TABLES Whatever the occasion or location I think round wedding tables look best-dressed when they are decorated with arrangements that are at different heights, so that the eye is drawn around the room. In grand ballrooms or marquees this is often achieved by using candelabras or tall fluted vases. For long tables, low arrangements can work well, but if the tables are a decent width you can also get some height by using candlesticks or taller containers. Long tables are mostly used to fit a large number of people into a room, and so are often narrow, and fill up quickly when you have added plates and two or three glasses to each place setting. One thing to bear in mind with low arrangements is that you do not want them to be too low or they will be hidden by the glasses, so vases at least 18cm (7in) tall are best. This is why footed glass bowls or urns are hard to beat as containers for events.

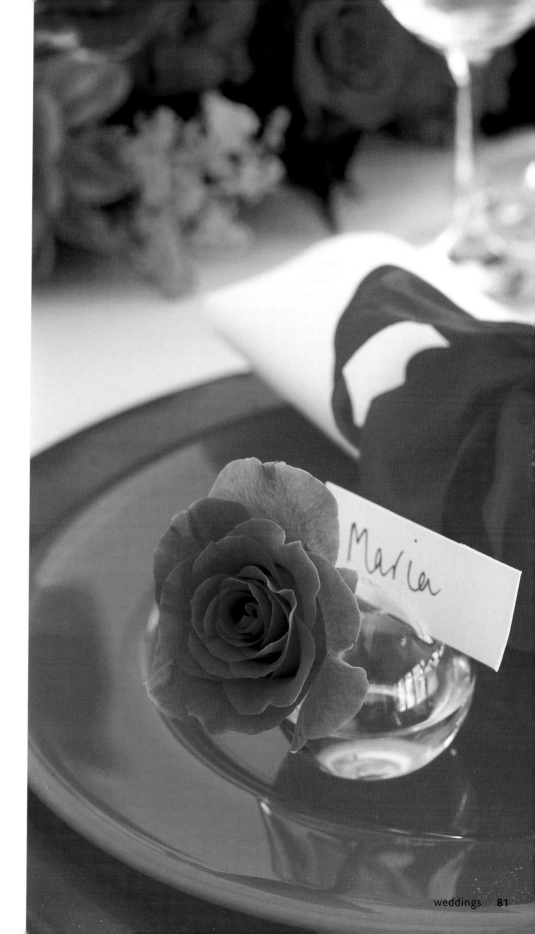

RIGHT Cerise wire-edged ribbon around each napkin and an individual bud vase with a cut to hold a name card; this is a pretty detail and a lovely keepsake or favour idea.

THIS PAGE AND OPPOSITE A bright pink glass cube vase is filled with a hand-tied bouquet of 'Milano' roses, *Alchemilla mollis*, echinops, gloriosa, *Brachyglottis* 'Sunshine', pink 'Karma Prospero' and 'Karma Choc' dahlias (a detail is shown left) and peonies.

ABOVE A 'Milano' rose edged with *Brachyglottis* 'Sunshine', pink hydrangea and eucalyptus flowers is secured with vibrant pink ribbon.

LEFT I find the delicacy of this 'Lyvera!' rose simply breathtaking. The pale tones of the ribbon and the napkin perfectly complement its ethereal beauty.

OPPOSITE Frosted pink ceramic vases are filled with pale pink 'Sarah Bernhardt' peonies, dahlias and sweet peas, mixed with *Alchemilla mollis* and hydrangea. Stems of pale pink *Clematis montana* var. *rubens* trail over the top for movement.

THIS PAGE A three-tier hexagonal pink wedding cake has been placed on two blocks of floral foam, separated from the icing on the cake by clear cellophane to keep the cake clean and avoid any contamination of the food. Often we would do this at the last minute and use dry green floral foam. The flowers will last at least five hours, maybe eight, depending on the temperature on the day. If you have to do this earlier and you want to use damp floral foam then remove it from the soaking bucket and let it dry out a little before using. When cutting the foam it is vital to make sure it is level to maintain stability, so a small builder's spirit level can be handy.

OPPOSITE The standard roses 'Blushing Akito', 'Belle Rose', 'Heaven!', 'Aqua!' and 'Lyveria!' have been mixed with the deep pink spray rose 'Magic Pepita'.

'The combination of pink icing and rosebuds
in every shade of pink is just divine — every
girl's dream of a fairytale wedding cake!'

'A baby girl —
the perfect excuse
for a pink party'

OPPOSITE Pale pink tulips, white sweet peas, honeysuckle and dill in a glass vase filled with alphabet sweets create a gorgeous scented spring offering. The palest pink mixes well with other pastel colours and this is one of the rare occasions when you find me mixing pale yellow with pink. I adore fuchsia pink with sunflower yellow, and I can work with pale pink and yellow, but somewhere in the mid colour range it can all go terribly wrong. So be wary of mixing pink with yellow unless it is in a vibrant multi-coloured assortment. Pink and yellow on their own do not always get on!

ABOVE Felted grey verbascum leaves are wrapped around glass votives tied with ribbon and topped with 'Anna' roses.

RIGHT These delicious hand-crafted rose petal bundt cakes come from the Ottolenghi food emporium in London.

children's parties

Children's parties, particularly for the under sevens, are currently going through a big revival. They are usually themed and an industry has grown out of the need to decorate the event. However, if all that manufactured plastic and paper gets you down you can find some simple and inexpensive ways to make your party look original, fresh and pretty.

DECORATING THE TABLE After you have chosen your theme then I would pick out your basics before selecting your flowers. There are great disposable napkins, cups and tablecloths available so you can easily find colours to complement your theme. I found these pink bugs on a flower wholesale internet site and my sundries wholesaler sells the pretty butterflies. Instead of covering the tops of the pink glass plant pot with moss I used some shredded pink paper, but you could also use highly coloured sisal, which is widely available from wholesale markets or even good stationers. I chose bubble-gum pink pelargoniums as they were the perfect colour, and also inexpensive, and they could be re-cycled after the event. The butterflies and bugs I re-use as present trim when I am wrapping gifts. Perfect for today's eco-conscious parents!

OPPOSITE A pink table with iced cakes, biscuits and pink milkshakes – sustenance for a group of apprentice fairies. The plastic chairs I bought in a yard sale; they were a municipal brown colour and so I spray-painted them pink. The paint ended up costing more than the chairs, but we had fun doing it and they look great!

BELOW Scrumptious homemade strawberry ice cream and berries with pink sugar crystals. I have been known to wander through Fortnum and Mason, the grand food store in London, wondering who needs sugar crystals in such a range of colours, but now I understand why.

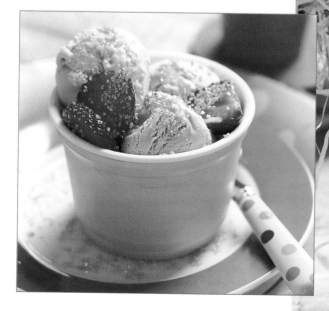

ABOVE These bugs came on bamboo canes and the butterflies were also wired, but you could easily wire them yourself so they can be arranged around a plant.

children's parties 95

ABOVE A pale pink iced cupcake with a silver foil-wrapped heart-shaped chocolate. What little girl could resist these treats?

RIGHT Pink glass flowerpots are filled with hand-tied posies of high summer garden blooms, including sweet peas, 'Dorothy Perkins' roses and lavender. Old glass jam jars edged with string are lined with pale translucent flower petals.

'Scented garden flowers and cupcakes are essential party pieces'

OUTDOOR EXTRAVAGANZA Children love eating outdoors, and it saves on the clearing up and mopping of the floors as you can leave all the crumbs for the birds! These little sand-filled glasses are a fun activity to do with little ones as it is easy and makes for a very attractive colourful container. It is best to invest in some plastic funnels so that the children will find it easier to place the sand between the glass and an inner plastic or paper cup. Colourful sand like this is easy to obtain as most pet shops have a wide variety in their aquatic departments. If you then fill the inner container with floral foam you could also get your little ones to fill them with flowers. Using foam is easier and more fun for children than attempting hand tying, and you may be surprised how successful their early attempts at floristry may be.

LEFT Gold confetti stars have been placed on the blue paper tablecloth to give the party a little more sparkle.

BELOW A small arrangement to top the cake has been created using the bottom of a polystyrene cup inset with a tiny block of foam, and then a few matching flower heads have been added.

For a children's summer outdoor birthday party, mixed posies of *Alchemilla mollis*, deep pink 'Beauty by Oger' roses, yellow achillea and bright pink 'Amalia' and 'Yellow Dot' spray roses have been placed in two glass tumblers. The smaller one inside holds the bouquet and the water, while swirls of brightly coloured aquatic grit to match the flowers have been carefully poured into the outer cavity.

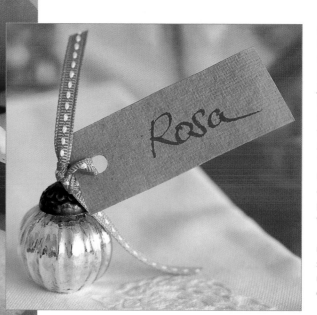

parties for grown-ups

Roses are the floral equivalent of the little black dress: they can be dressed up or down, and are the perfect choice for a grown-up party, whether it be an intimate get-together at home or a larger, catered event.

THE VERSATILITY OF PINK ROSES Throughout the pages of this book you will see at least 50 different shades of pink roses that we use. The small selection shown here is in the pale to dusty pink range, and then there are the more vivid and vibrant pinks such as 'Amalia', 'Tenga Venga', 'Poison' and 'Milano'. I love deep pink roses that are close to red and remind me of lipstick, such as 'Cherry Lady' and 'King Arthur'. I adore one or two bicolours en masse: 'Carousel' has a pale pink edge; 'N-joy' is darker and more vibrant. 'Blushing Akito' is the slightly deeper mid-pink sister of 'Sweet Akito' and as they are from the same family as the white 'Akito' they work well altogether in a pink and white theme. If you are using flowers in topiary then it is a good idea to use the same size flower head. At the smaller end of the scale you have 'Ballet', 'Heaven!' and 'Barbie', and at the largest end the aptly named 'Titanic'.

COCKTAIL HOUR There are so many great pink cocktails, with or without alcohol, that it is a great theme for a get-together to celebrate a birthday. Professionally, I am often asked to decorate cocktail parties and generally we do some large arrangements for the bar area and small arrangements for the occasional tables. At large cocktail parties the guests usually stand for the three hours they are sipping cocktails, and so it is better to have tall flowers on tables, pedestals or the bar where they can be admired. The flowers need to be above eye level to have impact. Simple but dramatic arrangements work best, and we very often work with lighting companies who give the odd wall or column a pink glow. Pink is a flattering, warming colour and works well in many different environments, from the modern to the classic.

RIGHT A flared pink glass table vase makes an elegant shape topped with a large ball of floral foam filled with a tightly massed mushroom shape of 'Sarah Bernhardt' and 'Karl Rosenfield' peonies and 'Milano', 'Belle Rose', 'Two Faces+' and 'Vendelle' roses.

OPPOSITE, LEFT 'Christian' spray roses are laid in a bright pink gift box lined with rosebud-sprigged Liberty fabric.

OPPOSITE, INSET Pomegranate Cosmopolitans and Strawberry Daiquiris are served on a pink tray, topped with kitsch but cool cocktail umbrellas, to get the party started.

ABOVE A small votive glass with galax leaf trim tied with pale pink aluminium wire is topped with a 'Bridal Kimsey' gerbera.

OPPOSITE AND LEFT These 'birthday cake' arrangements trimmed with candles are very popular for adult birthday parties. Pale pink 'Gerrie Hoek' dahlias and 'Bridal Kimsey' gerberas (detail shown left) along with 'Luxuria!' roses, are massed on a base of floral foam in a plastic tray. The container is edged with double-sided tape on which galax leaves are pressed, and secured with aluminium wire. Raised up on a footed pink cake stand and filled with small taper candles, it is just waiting for the birthday girl to make a wish.

afternoon tea

Stopping for afternoon tea on a regular working day is not something we tend to indulge in these days. But if you have something to celebrate, or want a focus when meeting up with a group of old friends, what could be nicer? It should be a civilized affair, with chintz, pretty china, lace tablecloths, meringues, strawberries, clotted cream and pretty cupcakes.

THIS PAGE A basket filled with carpet moss and topped with some old garden favourites, such as *Dianthus* 'Monica Wyatt', border spray carnations, chrysanthemums and some single pink Michaelmas daisies, with feverfew, *Alchemilla mollis* and a touch of double pink eustoma.

OPPOSITE These delicately speckled miniature strawberry and rose petal meringues are a perfect bite-sized treat at teatime, and they just look so pretty on a plate.

'Daisies, dianthus, strawberries and meringues — ingredients for the perfect summer tea'

EDIBLE TREATS The traditional value of afternoon tea mixes well with classical flowers or arrangements with a slightly retro feel. The comfort of a home-cooked iced cake needs to be matched with a simple arrangement of classic flowers. Basket arrangements, simple old-fashioned roses and arrangements with a light-hearted whimsical feel are just perfect for the revival of this enjoyable tradition. With or without tea, in the last five years there has been a huge resurgence of interest in the cupcake. They used to be decidedly an afternoon treat, but since cupcakes were immortalized in the TV drama *Sex and the City* where the girls enjoyed them at the now famous Magnolia Bakery in New York city, cupcake emporia have sprung up everywhere and eating them is no longer confined to afternoons. I think the attraction is in part the power of colour. Who can resist a pretty iced cake? It is decadence and fantasy in an individual paper wrapper. Visually pleasing, nostalgically reminiscent of more secure times, cupcakes are a kind of therapy on a plate, an instant pick-me-up from the trials of everyday life.

OPPOSITE 'Princess Alexandra' garden roses are massed together in a matching rubber vase. I really enjoy mixing the old with the new by taking an old-fashioned rose and putting it into a vase made from a vibrant new material.

RIGHT Frivolity and femininity are the hallmarks of this table setting. Delicate rose-pink icing forms a design on these miniature handbag biscuits, while heart-shaped sugar sprinkles in deeper shades echo the flamboyance of the roses.

LEFT When I spotted these ceramic pink waffle cone vases in a shop I thought they would be perfect for a floral take on the quintessentially English ice cream known as a '99', which consists of a chocolate flake placed into an ice cream cone. Here the appropriately named pink 'Barbie' and green 'Peppermint' roses have been arranged in foam to look like dollops of ice cream on a cone.

THIS PAGE This charming
oversized pink and white
spotted tea cup immediately
made me think of cream
'Talea+' and pink 'Belle Rose'
roses, whose colouring
perfectly reflects the container.

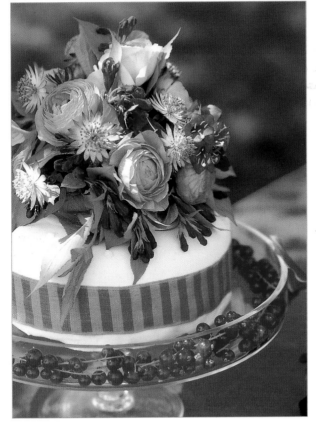

OPPOSITE Foam rings around huge storm lanterns make perfect centrepieces for this informal buffet table. Large-headed flowers such as peonies, lilies and the umbrella-shaped heads of dill are more striking for large arrangements than smaller-headed flowers.

TEA BENEATH THE TREES For this buffet table set out for a celebratory tea I chose a bright pink cloth to add a splash of colour to this green spot. Fruit trees, and in particular apple trees, are perfect for hanging votives as they generally have lots of low horizontal branches. We often use the orchard part of the garden for a feature because these trees look so stunning when they are twinkling in the late afternoon shadows. Bright pink votives add to the pink theme and look very pretty as the light falls and all the candles are lit. I particularly like to use scented flowers in my own home and an outdoor party is the perfect time to use flowers that might be quite overpowering in a confined space. Certain fragrances evoke memories and I adore the scent of large oriental lilies that remind me of my own wedding day.

ABOVE LEFT Cakes can be easily dressed up by adding a small floral arrangement to the top. Usually I place a small piece of floral foam in the bottom of a polystyrene cup. Here I have added weigela, ranunculus, astrantia and pale pink rose buds.

ABOVE RIGHT The strong colours of these deep pink lilies and chrysanthemums stands up well in bright sunlight, so they are perfect for outdoor arrangements.

afternoon tea   113

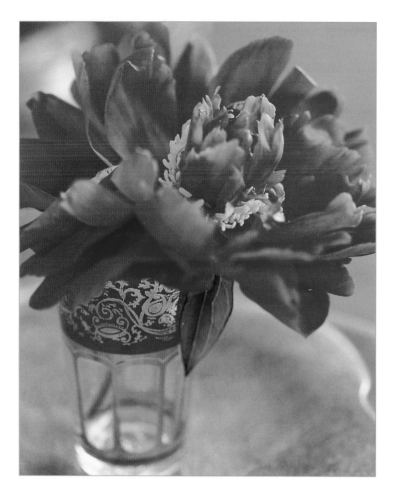

LEFT A blown 'Kansas' peony looks stunning in a matching pink tea glass.

BELOW Gold and pink is an unusual combination and gives a lovely light to any event. I am always on the lookout for small containers and shot glasses to make interesting votives.

OPPOSITE A floral ring around a glass bowl of floating candles is made up of grouped gloriosa, bright pink 'Milano' roses, 'Kansas' peonies, orange 'Colandro' roses, orange 'Tango' leucospermums, 'Lill Orange' zinnias and yellow *Achillea* 'Moonshine' with *Viburnum opulus* berries and *Corylus maxima* 'Red Filbert'.

dinner parties

Hot pinks are a great colour for dinner parties as they can be themed with the food and look good in candle or artificial light. Here, pink and gold Moroccan tea lights set the theme for a North African feast.

EXOTIC ELEGANCE Hot pink can look very sophisticated and I return often to this colour because it gives a cheerful and rosy glow to evening light. When it is used with other bold colours it can also be very masculine and so I think it suits lots of different occasions. Hot pink with purple and lime green has long been one of my favourite colour combinations and it is always a safe option, evoking memories of English country gardens. Using pink with orange and yellow requires rather more skill, and one tip is to use groups of colours as I have here, with berried foliages such as the *Viburnum opulus* and also some dark burgundy or brown foliages. Here the brown *Corylus maxima* 'Red Filbert' helps to make the bright combinations get along well together.

OPPOSITE *Achillea* 'Moonshine', orange zinnias and 'Colandro' roses with pink 'Milano' roses, gloriosa and celosia. The fluffy patches are the tops of *Cotinus*, or the smoke bush, which enhance the texture of this arrangement. This hand-tied posy is arranged in a moisture-containing pink gel that looks like ice, which is produced especially for the flower trade. I am not a huge fan of it, but like the ice effect of the clear gel and the pink is smart for dinner parties. Be very careful when you dispose of this gel because it is very absorbant and can block sinks and drains.

THIS PAGE One of my all-time favourite flowers has to be *Gloriosa superba* 'Rothschildiana' – it is a fantastic colour and shape, and often acts as a muse for my flower arrangement.

ROMANTIC DINNERS For Valentine's day over the years we have often used hat boxes as containers, which I think is a very smart way to receive a gift of flowers. Here the hat box is filled with an arrangement of hydrangea, roses and *Viburnum opulus* 'Roseum' to create a perfect pink centrepiece for a dinner party. Stemmed glass bowls and cake stands provide the perfect height for a dining arrangement as they elevate the flowers so that the glasses do not hide them, and still enable the guests to see across the table over the top of the flowers. It is important when planning an intimate dinner that the design does not create a hedge across the middle of the table and that arrangements are not intrusive. They should contribute to the romantic atmosphere, rather than hindering it!

THIS PAGE A glass cake stand has been filled with champagne-pink glass beads to hide the floral foam. *Viburnum opulus* 'Roseum' flower heads have been laid on the napkins and a dusting of pink petals strewn across the table. Stemmed bowls and cake stands also allow lots of space for votives, which adds to their suitability as containers for intimate dinners.

'*Candlelit tables on a balmy evening set the scene for a magical dining experience*'

OPPOSITE Black wrought-iron candelabra are the perfect height for a low centrepiece as they are footed and just tall enough to be seen above the wine and water glasses. Grapes have been wired into the bottom of these arrangements with 'Con Amore' roses, 'Cool Water!', 'Blue Pacific' and 'Christian' spray roses, along with *Heuchera* 'Plum Pudding' and *Cotinus coggygria* 'Royal Purple'.

THIS PAGE Napkins are trimmed with a 'Blue Pacific' rose and striped voile ribbon and laid on lilac glass charger plates.

techniques

hand-tied bouquets

When the stems are cleaned take one central flower between your thumb and your first finger so that it is resting on the palm of your hand. As I am right handed I arrange into my left hand so that my right is available for twisting the bunch and using the scissors for cutting the stems and tie. The second stem will be placed left of the first stem towards a 45-degree angle. After five flowers, use your right hand to twist the bunch and then add another five towards the left at the same angle. What starts off as a fan of flowers will become a spiralled bunch. Continue the same method, twisting as you go, until you have used all your flowers and you will have a lovely dome-shaped bunch. These 'Amalia' roses have then been tied where they were held, which is known as the 'binding point'.

THE PRINCIPLE OF hand tying material started with early farming when sheaves of wheat and barley were spiralled into bunches, which when tied would stand on their own stems and could be left in the field to dry in the sun after the summer harvest. Hand tying flowers began in continental Europe in the later part of the 20th century and was slowly introduced to the UK around 20 years ago; it has since become a familiar floral technique worldwide. It is worth spending a little time learning this skill, even if you do not plan to work commercially with flowers, because you can achieve a very sophisticated look with the minimum of effort. It may take you around three or so goes at spiralling the stems before you get the knack. The best way to begin is with a collection of straight-sided woody stems such as a dozen commercially grown roses. The trade secret to making a great spiralled bunch is all in the preparation. The stems must be cleaned thoroughly so that there is no foliage on the lower stems, and you can use a sharp vegetable knife to prize away any thorns from the stems.

ABOVE LEFT The average hand-tied bouquet consists of around 20 to 30 stems of flowers and foliages with around one third being foliage. Here a summer collection of garden roses, sweet peas and nigella shows the beginning of a foliage edging or collar. Pinkish dracaena leaves have been folded around the bouquet. You can see how the angle of the flowers gets greater – at the end the bouquet's flowers are nearer a 90-degree angle than the inner circle of 45 degrees.

BELOW LEFT This pastel hand-tied bouquet of gerberas, bergamot, celosia and roses has been edged with hosta leaves. You can also create a bubble by tying a square of strong cellophane around the straight cut stems and then filling it with water to create an aqua pack. This is the perfect wrapping for a hostess bouquet so that she does not have to search round for a vase just when her guests are arriving!

AN EMPLOYEE OF the Firestone tyre factory in the United States accidentally discovered floral foam. The widespread production of the green foam that holds water has now been taken over by the company called Smithers Oasis, and now the green foam has become synonymous with the name 'Oasis'. Its invention has radically changed the way flowers can be arranged. Usually it is sold in blocks about the size of a house brick, but you can get jumbo blocks for larger arrangements and a huge range of spheres, cones, rings and other more specific shapes. It is principally dark green, which is generally thought to be the best colour as it can be easily hidden by foliage. Do not use the brown foam, which is intended for dried flowers and is not so absorbent. Remember when using foam to soak it for about ten minutes, letting it naturally fall to the bottom of deep water in a bucket or sink. Wait to use the foam until you see that the air bubbles have ceased to rise. Never force it into the water as 'drowning' causes air locks to form in the middle. Use flower food as it will further improve longevity of the flowers and top up daily with water mixed with flower food. Never let the foam dry out, as it will start to draw the moisture from the flowers and literally suck the life out of your arrangement!

ABOVE LEFT Balls of foam are useful for formal structures, especially for weddings. When massing lots of flowers it is a good idea to cover the foam with 2.5cm (1in) chicken wire. You can see that this floral foam ball has a plastic mesh around it to prevent it from breaking up when all the flower stems are added. When creating an arrangement like this, cut the flower stems quite short, approximately 5cm (2in), to avoid them crossing in the centre of the foam ball. This vase has been filled with petals and cellophane and topped with 'Revival' roses.

BELOW LEFT Lime-green floral foam has been used here to create a candle arrangement. Make sure you use a lot of floral foam for a candle arrangement and that it rises at least 2.5cm (1in), preferably 5cm (2in) from the top of the vase so that you can add the flowers and foliage at right angles, as shown here. The candle has been anchored in with bamboo canes, sold in garden centres, or you can use kebab sticks. Floral foam tape secures the canes.

fixing with floral foam

THIS PAGE One of my favourite floral foam items are rings commonly sold as wreath frames for the sympathy flower trade. These plastic or Styrofoam backed pieces are fantastic for table centres as they come in a huge array of sizes and can be used around vases, storm lanterns and also candelabras. Here I have backed a 35-cm (14-in) ring with galax leaves and used cotinus, ornamental kales, hydrangea and gerberas for decoration. The glass doughnuts seen in the bowl filled with gerbera heads are also useful for floating flowers and protecting them from the heat and flame of lit floating candles.

ALTHOUGH FLORAL FOAM is a great invention, there are times when you need to use other methods. Arranging flowers in water with flower food will give better longevity than foam and so for contract flowers, arrangements for the summer or when we want to get the absolute maximum life from our flowers we may use methods other than foam. This can also be dictated by the flowers themselves – some varieties do not last well in foam. This especially applies to weak stems such as sweet peas or cosmos, and succulent ones such as tulips, hyacinths and other spring-flowering bulbs. Hollow stems such as amaryllis and hydrangea will also benefit from being arranged in water, as will thirsty drinkers such as anemones or sunflowers.

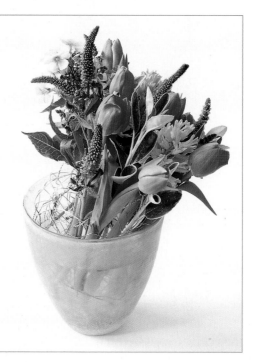

ABOVE RIGHT For larger vases, baskets and also large pedestals I use 5-cm (2-in) chicken wire to arrange flowers. I scrunch this up so that it fits the container so tightly you can pick up the vase by the wire.

BELOW I am not a great fan of floral gel, but as they make it in great colours, including pink, I thought it would be good to use it here. The gel is made by adding some crystals to water until it expands. As it contains water it allows the flowers to drink and because of its glutinous quality it keeps stems in place. The clear version is useful for creating an ice effect and gel is really a decorative accessory rather than a simple flower-arranging aid. These crystals last for ages, but are relatively expensive to purchase and have to be disposed of very carefully, as they can seriously block drains and sinks.

aids to arranging flowers

THIS PAGE If I am using a delicate shallow container I often use a grid of Sellotape or floral foam. Thin Sellotape works well for glass vases as it is see-through. I usually place all the horizontal pieces first and then add the vertical lines. For this arrangement I balanced bunches of delicate flowers such as the gypsophila with large flower heads of peonies and hydrangea.

decoration outside a container

THIS PAGE Double-sided tape has been attached around a straight-sided bowl and then sprigs of freshly cut 'Hidcote' lavender has been delicately placed around with the flower heads all at the same height. You can see that we have tied some string around it to assist us. Often we use a large rubber band on large bowls so that we can pull the band out to place each sprig in place behind it, stuck to the double-sided tape.

IF YOU DECORATE your container so that it is in sympathy with the flower arrangement you get a much more sculptural effect and this has become very much part of my signature style. In the days before there were so many floral accessories available, when I started my flower business, there were lots of ugly plastic containers on the shelves at the floral sundries stores. These seemed to me to be at complete odds with the beauty of the flowers. With a little double-sided tape and a few strong glossy leaves such as rhododendron, laurel, galax or even aspidistra you could transform your plastic inexpensively and quickly and make a natural container. Leaves last around five days before they start to get quite brittle, but mostly they dry out and look fine. For special occasions we have started to use herbs, and rosemary is one of the most versatile because it is available all year. Spruce works well for Christmas and, of course, the autumn leaves of oak are perfect. For winter we often get out the hot glue gun and stick cinnamon around plastic bowls. The only limit to this is your imagination and over the years we have tried a variety of natural items, from turnips and leeks to sunflower heads.

ABOVE LEFT With small containers such as votives you can often get away without using any tape by just wrapping three leaves around the outside, and using a decorative tie to keep the leaves in place. These skeletonized leaves are available in a number of dyed colours as well as natural forms.

BELOW LEFT Pink-dyed decorative twigs have been secured onto a glass vase with double-sided tape, trimmed to size and tied with fuchsia raffia.

decoration inside a container

BELOW Two straight-sided glass dishes have been placed inside one another to allow a small gap for a row of sweets. It is important that the gap is wide enough for one layer and not too wide as this makes the cost of the sweet filling more exorbitant than the flowers! Here I have used three blocks of coloured floral foam to fill the container. Notice that the foam rises about 5 cm (2in) above the container, which allows room for a generous amount of plant material and will allow flowers and foliages to be added at right angles so they hang over the edge of the container.

RIGHT The 15-cm (6-in) cube vase is one of my favourite containers. It is useful to buy a collection from 10 cm (4in) up to 20 cm (8in) so you use them in lots of different ways. Here decorative aggregate has been used. By using a central glass container you can add water with flower food to the centre vessel so that the grit does not get wet. This way it can be stored and re-used over and over.

BELOW A cylinder has been placed inside a fishbowl and then into the space swirls of pink dyed aquatic grit and paler pink coloured sand have been added in uneven stripes to evoke the waves of the sea. To achieve the best effect, with clearly delineated waves, use a funnel to pour the grit and sand into the narrow gap.

I HAVE ALWAYS LOVED to customize my own containers and over the years this has become quite a trademark. Initially I used plastic containers that were generally covered on the outside with double-sided tape, but as more and more fabulous glass shapes became available I started to use a container within a container to create lots of different effects. Sometimes the accessory can just add a colour, and coloured sand and aquatic grit – particularly for its garish colours – has been a huge favourite. Natural reeds and bamboos are great for simple table arrangements and fruit looks great for summer weddings, autumn events and, of course, Christmas, with cranberries or sliced oranges being my favourite. Spices such as star anise and cinnamon are also great for the festive season and give off a fabulous fragrance. For themed events, such as children's parties and christenings, I often like to use sweets, mainly because I am inspired by their colours!

BELOW Mikado sticks are generally natural and are used by florists in lots of different ways. Here pink dyed sticks have been used to line a container that has been filled with white floral foam to take lines of rose heads – a design suitable for a dining or coffee table. The foam and sticks have been cut just above the top of the container.

pink flower directory

pastel pinks

There are numerous shades of pastel pink flowers available all the year round, but many of my favourites are seasonal, and these are most prolific between the months of March and July.

Protea (left) The giant king protea is one of the largest pink flowers. Although they are quite expensive to purchase they are worth their cost because they last for a very long time and just a single stem in the right sturdy vase can cause quite a stir. We use them in contract vases, particularly in the summer, because they withstand hotter temperatures.

Valerian (1) This is actually a rather dominant self-sown plant in my garden, but I have come to adore these delicate flowers as fillers in bouquets and vase arrangements. This makes a better cut flower than you might expect if arranged in water with flower food.

Dog rose (2) These wild dog roses are a familiar site in hedgerows around the area where I live and they remind me very much of long hazy summer days in the country. Single roses have been having a little revival recently and apart from their wonderful shape I adore this shade of very pale pink.

Lupin (3) These quintessential garden flowers can often be overlooked as a cut flower because they do not travel very well and tend to drop quite easily. However I find if I cut them from my garden early in the morning and condition them with flower food they can easily last the best part of five days.

Clematis (4) Not yet grown in great numbers as a cut flower, the clematis has been sadly overlooked and rather underrated by the commercial flower industry. These flowers are lovely for wedding work and natural arrangements, when they can trail over the edge of vases and baskets. I like the strength of the vine and the leaf shape, too.

Anthurium (5) These funny looking waxy flowers usually divide people into the love or hate camp, but while I did not take enormously to the tropical red varieties I find myself increasingly beguiled by the new varieties and sizes, and I love their vase life habit of a minimum of 14 days to a maximum of 50!

Sweet pea (6) Fragrant and delicate, these flowers are among my top ten. Commercially grown sweet peas last longer than those cut from your garden because they are treated after they have been harvested. There is a huge variation in colours and also many bicolours. They last better in water than foam.

Hollyhock (7) This quintessential cottage-garden flower is grown in small quantities for the cut-flower industry and mainly double varieties are available for a limited season. Unfortunately this flower does not survive well as a cut flower and so I use them only for large arrangements for special occasions such as weddings, and I admire them in my garden.

Cymbidium orchid (8) These strong, long-lasting flowers are at their best in the winter and come in a huge range of pinks. The noses are most often burgundy and all have a touch of yellow. The large-headed varieties have 20 or so heads on the stem and can be as long as 80cm (2½ft).

Honeysuckle (9) No garden would be complete in my opinion without at least one variety of this plant and I have at least five different varieties so that I can enjoy this sweet musky fragrance for longer. Not a great cut flower, it will not survive floral foam, but it is lovely for special occasions.

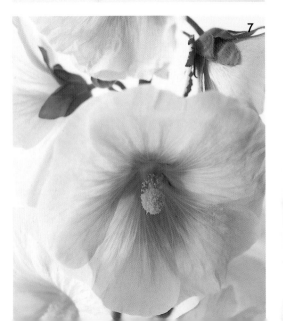

bright pinks

My favourites in the pink palette are the showy, loud pinks that make a strong visual statement.

Celosia (left) The vivid rich colours of celosia and their lovely texture provide interest in densely packed bouquets and arrangements. In early summer huge heads of celosia on giant stems are gown around San Remo in Italy and these are fantastic for pedestal designs and large-scale arrangements.

Peony (1) Peonies are quintessential blowsy showy pink flowers and have the added advantage of being fragrant. 'Karl Rosenfield' and 'Kansas' are two of my favourite bright pink varieties to use as long-lasting cut flowers.

Rhododendron (2) For a very short season in spring I love to use the beautiful flowers from these magnificent shrubs. Their close relatives the azaleas sport some beautiful blossoms and also some pretty racy pink colours.

Stock (3) This old-fashioned gillyflower has been a cottage garden favourite for centuries, but has now been much improved. Most widely available is the bright pink *Matthiola incana* 'Francesca'. Pictured here is 'Lucinda Rose'.

Gerbera (4) These are very versatile flowers available in a huge palette of pink. Among the large flower varieties 'Serena' pictured here is the most common and 'Whisper' and 'Leila' are my favourite mini gerberas.

Dianthus (5) The standard carnations come in a huge array of pink colours and I love the ones that are the closest to purple. 'Farida' shown here is almost the colour of beetroot. Massed together, standard carnations are very textural and I prefer to use them cut short in domed hand-tied bouquets.

Phalaenopsis orchid (6) Beautiful moth-shaped flower heads in a huge spectrum of bright pink colour. On long drooping stems they make exotic but simple bridal bouquets or luxurious vase arrangements. Usually quite pricy, they last incredibly well and so are better value than you might think.

Tulip (7) There are a huge variety of pink tulips, including the later flowering 'Pink Diamond', the fringed 'Huis ten Bosch' and the lily-flowering 'China Pink'. Versatile and easy to use, tulips grow around a third more after they have been cut, so allow for a little movement when mixing with other flowers.

Dahlia (8) I adore dahlias for their colour and their texture. The Karma series has several pinks and are long-lasting cut flowers. *Dahlia* 'Onesta' is another fine showy pink dahlia. I look out for the Cactus varieties, such as 'Pink Jupiter' or 'Pink Symbol'.

Fuchsia (9) No discussion on showy pink flowers should leave out fuchsias, which have so aptly left their mark on the colour pink by defining one of its best palettes. Not reliable at all as a cut flower, but an essential part of a British summer either in the garden and on the patio or hanging from a basket in your favourite municipal English park.

1

2

3

4

5

6

7

8

9

mixed pinks

Two-tone pinks are lovely for monochromatic and complementary combinations, and can be visually stunning when arranged on their own.

Nigella (left) I saw this exciting new variety, 'Power Pink', for the first time as a cut flower while we were making this book. The blue cultivar is the traditional colour and a cottage garden favourite. I love nigella for weddings in the summer.

Gladioli (1) Loved or hated, this sturdy flower is great for large pedestals and for massing in vases. The bicolours and the stronger pinks are my favourites and they last extremely well.

Zantedeschia (2) Known more commonly as arum or calla lilies, these elegant long-lasting versatile flowers are the super models of the flower industry. They are the flower of choice for many floral designers, so they can usually command high rates because they are always in demand.

Digitalis (3) From late April to May, foxgloves grow wild in woods and are very precious to me. I grow some cultivars in my garden and make the most of the limited supply of cut foxgloves when they are in season in May.

Dianthus (4) These old-fashioned cottage garden 'pinks' have a divine scent and have been admired in English gardens since Tudor times. Their more common supermarket sisters always seem to get a bad press nowadays, but they are hard-working and faithful flowers.

Gloriosa (5) This is another top ten flower. I just love its shape, its colour and it is definitely a muse for my inspiration. The bicolour often leads me to use pink with yellow or lime green to some stunning, vibrant effects. It is also another great favourite of mine for use in dramatic wedding arrangements.

Lily (6) There are so many great pink oriental lilies around and I always like to have a vase on the go at home. They last for up to two weeks and they give off a divine sweet smell that reminds me of my wedding day.

Mallow (7) This lowly common pink flower often found on roadsides or wastelands has many famous pink relatives, from the lofty hollyhock to the tropical hibiscus. It has beautiful delicate rose-purple flowers which have been admired since the 8th century, and has been used widely as a medicine and a food as well as a cut flower.

Astrantia (8) Some flowers are all about the colour, others scent, but this one is all about the texture. The delicate umbrella-shaped heads make great supporting actresses to roses in summer wedding bouquets. They enhance other shapes and last well themselves.

Rose (9) There are lots of bicolour roses from the garden as well as commercially grown cultivars. In my garden I grow 'Handel' around an arch and favourites that are commercially grown include the small-headed rose 'N-joy' and the large-headed 'Dolce Vita'.

1

2

3

4

5

6

7

8

9

index

Figures in italics refer to captions.

acknowledgements

This book has been an absolute pleasure to work on. It has been a long time in the pipeline, so there has been a huge team that has worked on it or were involved from its conception to its birth. A huge thank you to Jacqui Small, my publisher, for giving me the opportunity to indulge my love of pink! Thanks to her efficient and artistic team, which includes as usual the talented and patient designer Maggie Town, the very capable and knowledgeable skills of my editor Sian Parkhouse, Lesley Felce and all at Jacqui Small who lent pink props, shared pink insights and loves and added to the passion for this book as well as to the organization.

A very special thank you to all the photographers who have worked on these pink designs including Sian Irvine and Sarah Cuttle and a very big thank you to Polly Wreford who shot the body of new work for this special and very personal book. Polly and I had worked together once before about 20 years earlier when we were both starting out on our careers and it was an immense privilege and fun to work with her on this project. As usual in publishing these days she had to achieve a lot in a very short time, which required immense skill, vision, speed and patience. Heartfelt thanks to Polly and her assistant Sarah.

Over the last 20 years I have had the pleasure to work with lots of lovely talented florists and we have also trained and added to the experiences of many along the way. During the production of this book I have had the pleasure to work with the following talented people: Wendy Boileau, Heidi Bradshaw, Anne Cadle, Katie Cochrane, Kirsten Dalgleish, Yolanda Davis, Steve Dzingel, Anita Everard, Jason Fielding, Samantha Griffiths, Anna Hudson, Gina Jay, Shontelle Jepson, Anita Kovacevic, Hyunah Lee, Hyun Sook Lee, Su Yeon Lee, Miranda Laraso, Sarah Laugher, Estelle Montlouis, Gillian Munday, Annabel Murray, Tania Newman, Phil O'Neil, Penny Pizey, Ann Pochetty, Hayley Pryke, Joanne Rouse, Chris Sharples, Miki Tanabe, Viktor Tordai, Natasha Tshoukas, Vilija Vaitilaite, Hisako Watanabe, Karen Weller, Kate Wozniak and Jisook Yim.

Thank you to our cake bakers Fiona Cairns, Penny Pizey, Gerhard Jenne and the team at Ottolenghi. Thanks to Anne Cadle for the lovely pink wedding cake on page 86. Thanks to Aline Johnson, Isobel Stanley and Emma Bridgewater for their creative containers.

My long-standing flower suppliers: in particular in New Covent Garden market and also in the Netherlands. Dennis at John Austin and Co, Marcel from MHG flowers and Kees and Jack from Ros flowers. The team at Bloomfield, everyone at Best, Whittingtons and Pratleys.

Last but by no means least, a very special thank you to my family who have contributed so much to this project and who are a constant support. Thank you for your love and encouragement.

picture credits